TO THE RESCUE!

Ambulances
to the Rescue
Around the World

Linda Staniford

raintree

a Capstone company — publishers for children

Raintree is an imprint of Capstone Global Library Limited, a company incorporated in England and Wales having its registered office at 264 Banbury Road, Oxford OX2 7DY – Registered company number: 6695582

www.raintree.co.uk
myorders@raintree.co.uk

Edited by Linda Staniford
Designed by Steve Mead
Picture research by Eric Gohl
Production by Victoria Fitzgerald
Originated by Capstone Global Library Ltd
Printed and bound in China

ISBN 978 1 474 71524 9
20 19 18 17 16
10 9 8 7 6 5 4 3 2 1

British Library Cataloguing in Publication Data
A full catalogue record for this book is available from the British Library.

Acknowledgements
We would like to thank the following for permission to reproduce photographs:
Alamy: CulturalEyes - AusGS2, 4, Leila Cutler, 17; AP Photo: State Journal/Craig Schreiner, 16, 22 (top); Ellie Kealey Photography: 15; Getty Images: AFP/Peter Martell, 14, Bergwacht Bayern, 19; iStockphoto: Giambra, 7, Liz Leyden, cover, ollo, 11, sturti, 6, swalls, 8; Newscom: Image Broker/Jochen Tack, 5, Robert Harding,/ Ken Gillham, 12; Shutterstock: Alexander Tolstykh, back cover (left), 13, 22 (bottom), CandyBox Images, 20, i4lcocl2, back cover (right), 18, michaeljung, 21, My Life Graphic, 10, 22 (middle), Tim Large, 9

Design Elements: Shutterstock

Every effort has been made to contact copyright holders of material reproduced in this book. Any omissions will be rectified in subsequent printings if notice is given to the publisher.

All the internet addresses (URLs) given in this book were valid at the time of going to press. However, due to the dynamic nature of the internet, some addresses may have changed, or sites may have changed or ceased to exist since publication. While the author and publisher regret any inconvenience this may cause readers, no responsibility for any such changes can be accepted by either the author or the publisher.

Contents

Some words are shown in bold, **like this**.
You can find out what they mean by looking
in the glossary.

What are ambulances?

Ambulances are **emergency** vehicles that are used all over the world. They help people who need **medical** treatment.

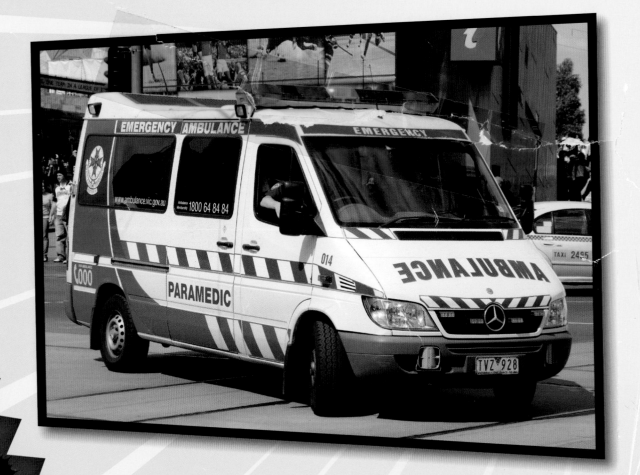

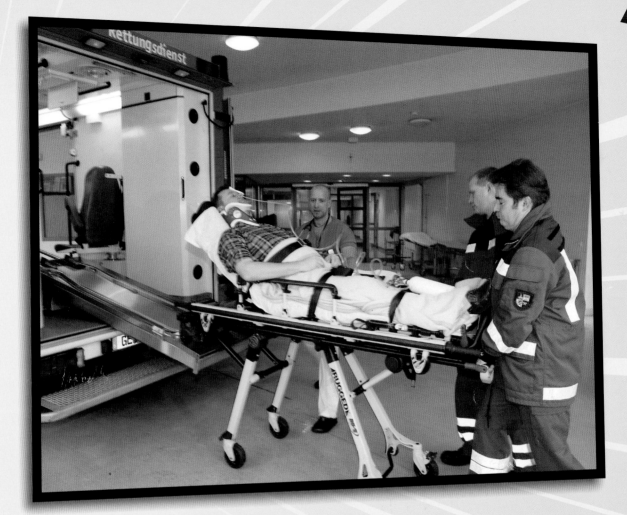

If someone is seriously injured or has an
illness that can't be treated at home,
we call an ambulance. The ambulance
arrives and takes the person to hospital.

Who drives ambulances?

The crew of an ambulance are called paramedics. In some countries they wear **uniforms**.

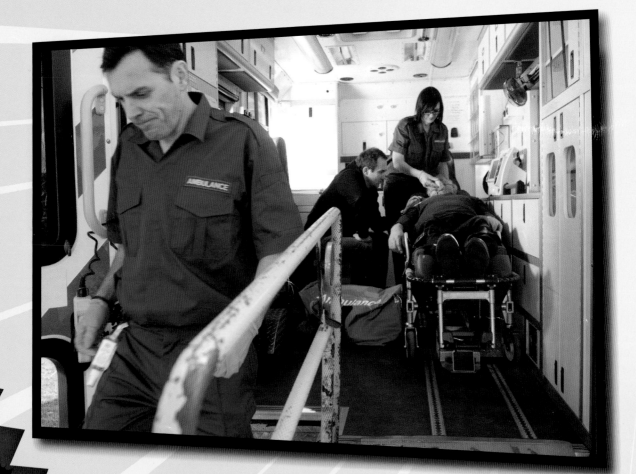

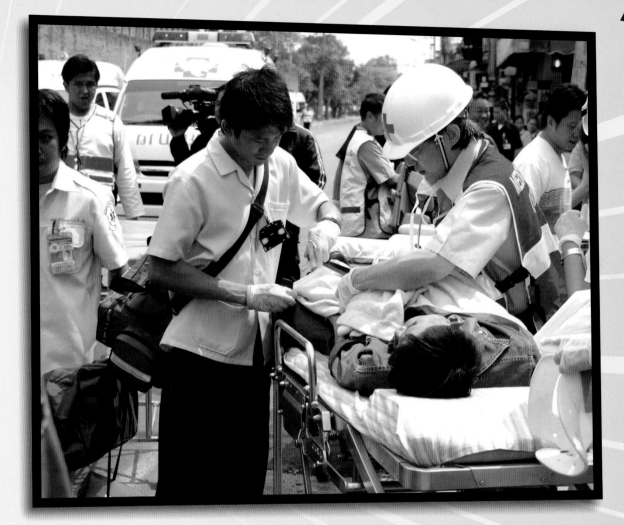

Paramedics can deal with all kinds of **medical emergencies**. Often they can treat people without having to take them to hospital.

What do ambulances look like?

Ambulances are often painted a bright colour such as white, yellow or red. They have a blue or red flashing light and a **siren**.

Some paramedics travel in an **emergency** response car. They can begin to treat the injured person before the ambulance arrives.

What is inside an ambulance?

Ambulances carry lots of different **equipment**. They have stretchers to carry injured people, bandages to treat wounds, and oxygen tanks.

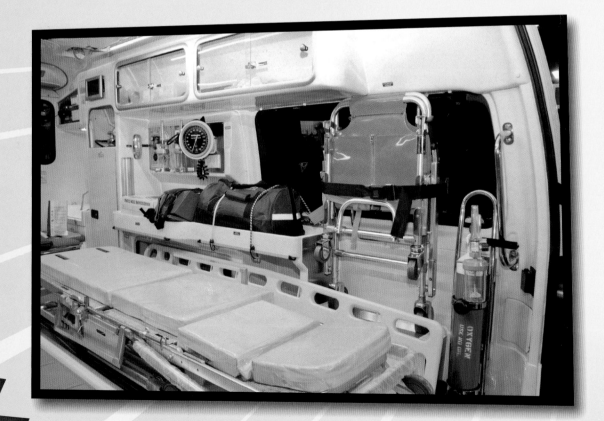

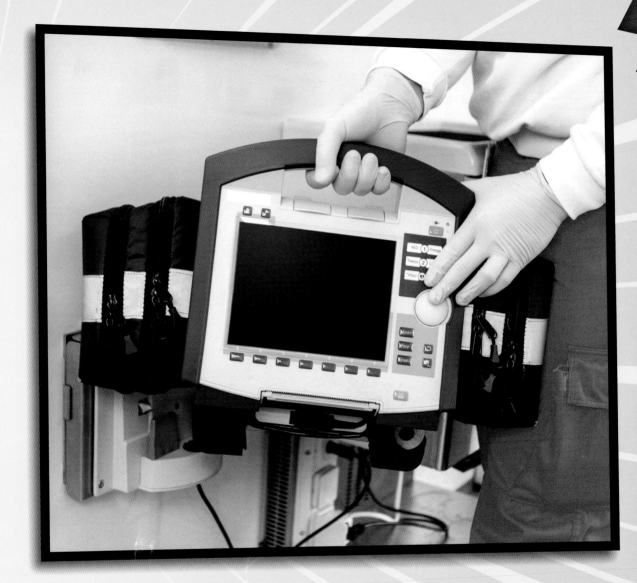

Ambulances also have a **defibrillator**.
This can restart a person's heart if the
heart has stopped beating.

How are ambulances different around the world?

In Australia, ambulances need to travel over long distances where there are no roads. The Flying Doctor service uses planes and helicopters to reach people who need **medical** help.

In Venice, Italy, people travel on **canals** instead of roads. Boats called water ambulances take people to hospital.

In South Sudan, Africa, motorcycle ambulances are used to reach people on roads big ambulances can't reach. They have a **side car** for an injured person to ride in.

In Afghanistan, donkey ambulances are used to take people to health centres. The donkeys have a padded seat on their backs to carry the sick person over **rough** ground.

Can ambulances travel on mountains?

Some special ambulances can travel on snow and ice. In Switzerland these ambulances have runners like skis. They can cross ice to rescue people who are injured while skiing.

In Bulgaria there are ambulances that run on **tracks** instead of wheels. They can climb up snowy mountains to reach injured climbers.

What if ambulances can't get through?

Helicopters are used to reach people who are injured on mountains or clifftops where there are no roads. This service is called the Air Ambulance.

People can get injured when they explore caves deep underground. Paramedics use special **equipment** to rescue injured people from the caves.

Making the world a safer place!

Ambulance crew have a very exciting and **rewarding** job. They help sick and injured people every day. They never know what might happen next.

Ambulance crew are very brave people. It is good to know we can call them if there is an **emergency**.

Quiz

Question 1
What kind of ambulances can run on snow and ice?
a) helicopters
b) motorcycles
c) ambulances with runners or tracks

Question 2
Which of these are found in an ambulance?
a) stretcher
b) bicycle
c) horse

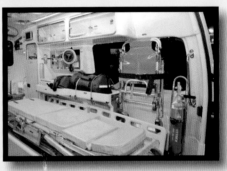

Question 3
What kind of ambulances would you find in Venice?
a) Flying Doctor
b) water ambulances
c) donkey ambulances

Glossary

canal human-made waterway

defibrillator piece of medical equipment that applies an electric shock to restart the heart

emergency sudden and dangerous situation that must be handled quickly

equipment machines and tools needed for a job or an activity

medical to do with helping sick or injured people get better

rewarding worthwhile

rough not smooth

side car small car attached to one side of a motorcycle

siren device that makes a loud sound

track piece of metal and rubber that stretches around a vehicle's wheels

uniform special clothes that members of a particular group wear

Find out more

Books

Emergency 999! Ambulance, Kathryn Walker (Wayland, 2013)

First Book of Emergency Vehicles, Isabel Thomas (A&C Black, 2014)

People who Help Us: Ambulance Crew, Honor Head (Wayland, 2013)

Websites

Find out more about ambulances and paramedics here:
http://www.ambulance.nsw.gov.au/Kids-Stuff.html

Games and quizzes from an Australian ambulance service about accidents, paramedics and how to stay safe:
http://www.funkidslive.com/features/professor-halluxs-map-of-medicine/paramedic%E2%80%99s-ambulance

Index